Quick SAP Basic Introduction End User Guide

Learn SAP GUI Navigation, Reports, Tips and Tricks with Basic SAP Skills

SYED AWAIS RIZVI

PUBLICATIONS

Copyright © 2015 Syed Awais Rizvi

Author: **Syed Awais Rizvi**

Executive Project Manager: Syed Imon Rizvi and Adeel Mehdi

Senior SAP Architect: Ali Zer Rizvi

SAP Consultant: Muhammad Osaja Rizvi

Production Manager: Syed Ali Qasim and Raza Naqvi

Project Director: Syed Mohammed Saqib Zaidi

Copyright © 2017 Syed Awais Rizvi

All rights reserved.
Paperback Edition
ISBN: 1542515602
ISBN-13: 978-1542515603
Kindle eBook
ISBN-10:1942554044
ISBN-13:978-1942554042

DEDICATION

I dedicate this book to my parents for their love and support.

ACKNOWLEDGMENTS

الحمد لله ربّ العالمين

I would like to thank my mother and father for the support. My book would not have been possible without amazing support of my wife Sairah. I would like to thank my family for the support and love. I would like to thank my brothers Imon Rizvi for always encouraging words. I would like to thank my beloved teacher Ustad Sibtay Jaffer for his kind guidance and devoted support. Ustad Sibtay Jaffer is a living example for all of his students and community for his humbleness, kindness and intellectual noble contributions.

The most forgiving person is one who forgives in spite of his ability to punish. (or avenge)

Saying of Imam Hussain a.s

Improve SAP Skills

- **Learn SAP Basics and Improve Productivity**

  From this book user can gain an edge of improved transactions in SAP. All of little task where we can manager something faster and automation will improve productivity. From book use automatic parameters for transaction to auto populate entries.

- **Improve SAP Navigation Skills**

  SAP navigating skill represent very important for new and current users to learn. Shortcuts with the knowledge of shortcuts and customization users utilize system mush faster.

- **Favorites transaction code List**

  Favorite transaction code list make easy buttons for users to click on transaction and also no longer require users to remember transaction codes.

- **Automate SAP Default Entries**

  With parameters entry can be entered automatically. If user use specific one order type or sales organization frequently then the values will be automatically entered.

- **SAP GUI Color Customization**

  GUI color can be customized. Learn step by step guide how to modify SAP GUI color.

- **Customize User Defaults for Date and Number**

  Learn how to customize numbers and date in SAP.

- **Learn SAP ALV Report Tricks**

  SAP ALV report render control of adjusting columns, display, filter and save adjusted custom layout of the report.

- **Find All Available Standard Report**

Find all possible reports from SAP.

- **Learn SAP Error and Massages**
  Learn about SAP massages and their meaning to interpret error. Learn visual errors from SAP.

Why This Book?

End users to improve their SAP GUI and navigation skills. In many projects end users lack knowledge with SAP GUI functions. Users, consultants and beginners also improve their basic skills in SAP GUI. SAP GUI derive with huge amount of functions and book focused on most utilized functions. This Book focused on most utilize and productive functions for end users to improve productivity.

Who is this book for?

- End User
- Consultants
- Business Analysts
- Managers
- Beginners
- SAP ABAPER (Programmer).

Quick SAP Basic Introduction End User Guide for anyone new, experienced or anyone want to improve their basic SAP GUI skills.

Disclaimer:

This publication contains references to the products of SAP AG.

SAP, R/3, SAP NetWeaver, Duet, PartnerEdge, ByDesign, SAP BusinessObjects Explorer, StreamWork, and other SAP products and services mentioned herein as well as their respective logos are trademarks or registered trademarks of SAP AG in Germany and other countries. Business Objects and the Business Objects logo, BusinessObjects, Crystal Reports, Crystal Decisions, Web Intelligence, Xcelsius, and other Business Objects products and services mentioned herein as well as their respective logos are trademarks or registered trademarks of Business Objects Software Ltd. Business Objects is an SAP company. Sybase and Adaptive Server, iAnywhere, Sybase 365, SQL Anywhere, and other Sybase products and services mentioned herein as well as their respective logos are trademarks or registered trademarks of Sybase, Inc. Sybase is an SAP company. SAP AG is neither the author nor the publisher of this publication and is not responsible for its content. SAP Group shall not be liable for errors or omissions with respect to the materials. The only warranties for SAP Group products and services are those that are set forth in the express warranty statements accompanying such products and services, if any. Nothing herein should be construed as constituting an additional warranty.

This book is written by Syed Rizvi with his own personal views and understanding, it is not representing any company, products, and registered trademark. The author do not assume no responsibility on error and omissions, book is based on "AS-IS". All the screenshot are copyright by SAP AG. This publication expresses no warranty, damages, guaranty, and liability whatsoever professional or any kind, direct or indirect. This book does not express warranty or guaranty, articulated or indirect to the accurateness or comprehensiveness of any information published herein of any kind.

Contents

Improve SAP Skills v

CHAPTER 1 12

Introduction to SAP 12
   Introduction to SAP: 13
   SAP Three Tire System: 13
   Application Server: 16
   Presentation: 17
   Database Server: 17
   SAP Modules: 18
   SAP Finance FICO: 19
   MM Material Management / WM Warehouse Management 20
   SAP Sales and Distribution: 21
   PP Production Planning: 23
   GTS and GTM 24
   SAP GRC: 25
   SAP Activate 25
   Agile Methodology: 26
   ASAP Implementation Methodology: 26
   Project Preparation: 27
   Objective: 28
   Blueprinting: 28
   Blueprint Documents: 29
   Realization: 30
   Go-live Preparation and Go-live 31
   Best Practices: 31
   SAP Configuration: 32
   OSS Notes: 33
   EHP: 34
   SAP Fiori: 34
   SAP Personas: 34
   Project: 35
   Project Phases 37
   Project Issue / Opportunity Management: 38
   Issue Log: 39

Project Risk Management:...39

PMO:..40

Project complete life cycle:...40

SOW:...41

Lesson learned Project Experience:...42

IT Infrastructure:..43

Rationale Document:...43

Enterprise:..44

ECC:...45

Service Pack:...45

System Landscape:...45

Development System:...46

Quality System:...46

Production System:..47

ABAP:...47

ALV:..47

BAPI:..48

Document:..48

Field:..52

Data in SAP...55

Master Data:..55

Node:..55

EDI:..56

IDOC:..56

SQL...56

ANSI...56

BASIS...56

Instance..57

Server..57

IP address..57

Object:..57

Synchronous Interface:..58

Asynchronous Interface:..58

AR (Account Receivable) and AP (Account Payment):.............................58

Accrual and cash Basis Accounting:..58

Profit Center:...58

Cost Center:...58

Process:...59

Business Process:..59

Process Flow Diagram:..59

Workflow..60

Use case: 61

General Ledger Accounting: 62

T-Account: 62

WBS: 63

Journal entry: 63

Credit 64

Debit 64

Debit and Credit: 64

SAP Consultant: 65

OCM: 65

Stake Holder: 65

Big Data 66

"Z" and "Y" customization: 66

Role and Responsibility: 66

CHAPTER 2 ....**68**

SAP Navigation **68**

SAP GUI: 69

.SAP GUI Setup: 70

SAP Easy Access Menu: 71

T-code: 72

Tips to remember T-code: 72

T-code Bar: 73

Transaction Code Short Cuts: 74

SAP Copy Past: 75

Easy Access Menu buttons and shortcuts: 76

SAP Messages T 78

SAP Massage Type 79

Changing GUI Color 80

Quick Copy Past 81

SAP Print Screen: 82

Transaction Desktop Shortcut 83

Add Favorite T-codes: 83

T-code Name Display: 84

Personalize and Defults Setup **85**

Date format: 85

Automatic Populated Values 87

Parameter ID Automatic Defaults: 87

List of useful parameters: 88

Display Dropdown Keys: 89
Search Transaction Code 90
Show Keys in Dropdown List: 92

CHAPTER 3 94

SAP Reports and Layout: 94
ALV: 95
SAP Report Selection: 95
Reports: 96
View from Report 97
Change from Report: 97
Report Ascending and Descending: 98
Filter in Report: 98
Total in Report: 98
Change Layout 99
Save Layout 99
Select Layout 100
Download Local File 100
Print Preview 102
Report Customization: 102

About The Author 104

Chapter 1

Introduction to SAP

Introduction to SAP:

SAP AG represents a name of German Software Company. SAP commonly known for ERP application. SAP stands for System Application Product in data processing. SAP ERP encompass modules for each business department. The modules represent independent business departments. The functions of business units represented in modules. SAP Modules tightly integrates with other modules with centralization of master and transnational data. SAP ERP modules integration centralized business functions.

SAP ERP constituent a suite of integrated modules, which together accommodate business process. The modules designed with the best practices and "industry standard." The "IS" aberration apply for industry enhanced version. Following represents examples of the IS solutions:

IS-Retail
IS-Oil and Gas
IS-Auto

SAP Three Tire System:

The industry solution provides in-depth features and functions that able to benefit the system readiness with fewer enhancements. IS-Auto industry provide solutions in parts suppression, including VIN tracking the whole life cycle of VIN management. SAP Out of the box requires customization according to the company's needs and activation of industry's best practices. SAP features suites of software products available. The latest version of SAP ERP's called "SAP ECC ERP," that stands for ERP Central Component. SAP ERP represent three-tier based system with each tier representing each section of the software application.

- Application (Application Server)
- Presentation (Computer, mobile, web, etc.)
- Database (Database server)

Subsequent Figure Present the three-tier system.

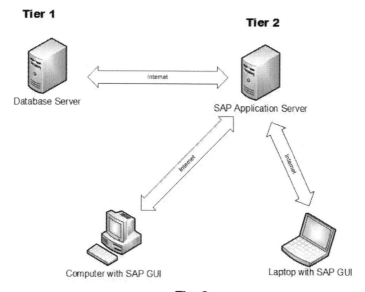

Figure 1

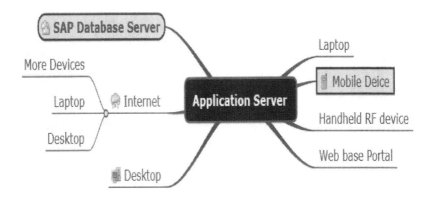

Figure 2

Application Server:

The SAP Application server represent part of the R/3 architecture. A virtual server or physical server represent a machine that feature multiple processors that handles multiple programs at a time. A SAP application server is accessed via the GUI. The server able to then connect too many devices including the presentation tier and connect with SAP database server, completing the three tier systems of SAP ERP R/3.

Presentation:

Presentation present the SAP GUI software that installed on to computer or laptop. GUI stands for graphical user interface. The Presentation tier able to utilize via mobile or web browser. The device that connected to the application server via GUI or web or mobile device called presentation.

Database Server:

The database represent a collection of tables. The collection of many tables together on the same sever called database. Once the collection of tables saved in the database server then server process with application server. The database server comprise one server or expected to represent a grouped on servers that represent the database. The SAP ERP database server feature a separate server.

SAP Modules:

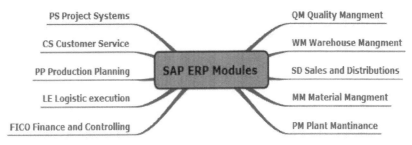

PS Project Systems		QM Quality Mangment
CS Customer Service		WM Warehouse Mangment
PP Production Planning	**SAP ERP Modules**	SD Sales and Distributions
LE Logistic execution		MM Material Mangment
FICO Finance and Controlling		PM Plant Mantinance

Figure 3

SAP application constitute a solution for enterprise. Enterprise consists of many departments and SAP ERP solution divided in to modules for the different department. Any business expected to divide into three main units:

- Accounting

- Human resource

- Logistics

These departments able to divided into many more sub divisions. The sub division of these main unites of business are represented as modules in SAP. Each module expected to standalone implemented with integration other systems. SAP modules are integrated and communicate to each other seamlessly. The following represent samples of SAP modules:

SAP Finance FICO:

FICO stands for finance and controlling (modules). SAP FI and CO represent two different modules but heavily integrated with each other. Each business entity requires accounting setup for the legal and internal process. For example some functions comprise of general ledger reporting, tax, account receivable, account payable, and so on The FI module feature a factory calendar, GL General Leger account, chart of account, company code (separate entity), reconciliation account, account payable, account, and receivable account groups among more functions. Integration point of SAP SD and SAP FI embody at the sales order level at sales, customer master payment method and, payment term; it also integrates at for credit management for customer credit master. SAP FICO Finance integrates at account determinations, revenue determination, cost center, and costing.

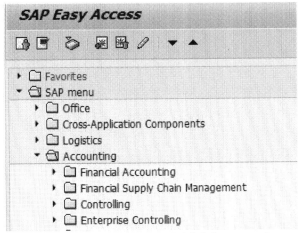

Figure 4

MM Material Management / WM Warehouse Management

Material management module represent part of logistics. Material management involves inventory and purchasing process, subcontracting, procurement, etc. The warehouse management module represent part of material management module. WM module embody a sub-part of the material management module. The WM module features major activities involved in plant and warehouse related transactions. The process under WM comprise of cycle counting, inventory management, transfer order, picking order, picking, packing, handling unit, etc.

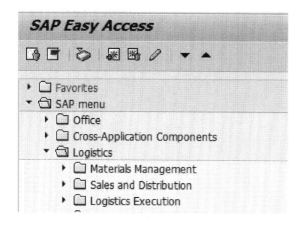

Logistic Execution:

The SAP Logistic Execution module integrates sales and distribution along with the material management module. The distribution channel present one of the integration points between SAP SD and logistic execution. The enterprise structure configuration represent in the logistic execution area. Cash cycle delivery document follow another point of integration with logistic execution. Delivery inbound and outbound process come under logistic execution.

Following represent few of logistic execution related functionalities:

- Inbound Delivery
- Outbound Delivery
- Warehouse Management
- Shipping
- Yard Management

SAP Sales and Distribution:

SAP Sales and distribution module feature functionalities that consist of sales related activities. Sales functionalities include inquiry, quotation, contracts, pricing, sales orders, billing, rebate, and many more.

Pricing:

Pricing represent one of the complex functions of sales and distribution module that support many scenarios. Pricing is also utilize in the material management module with the same basic principle.

Sales order:

Sales order management and configuration control, inquiry, quotation, order on key areas of sales and distribution module.

Delivery:

Delivery comprise in the integrated areas of the logistic execution module including the sales and distribution stand point customization of outbound delivery.

Billing:

Billing integrate Finance and sales and distributions modules. Billing account determination and bling plans are customized. Billing completes order to cash cycle.

Credit Management relates to the customer master data setup and also finance integrated areas to setup credit master.

To view sales and distribution related T-codes:

VA00 will bring only sales related menu from an easy access menu
VF00 will display all billing related t-codes

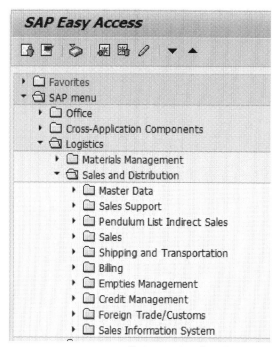

PP Production Planning:

The PP module provides product production planning,

controlling, and scheduling. It involves, bill of material, long term planning, demand management, material requirement planning, capacity planning, production orders, and KANBAN process.

GTS and GTM

SAP Sales and Distribution feature standard trade compliance functionalities, which is outdated and limited. SAP GTS and GTM modules feature full range of functionality with industry standards best practices. SAP GTS stands for Global Trade Compliance. SAP GTM stands for Global Trade Management. SAP GTM manages compliance from the standpoint of globally. SAP GTS integrates the logistics and financial areas to custom compliances. SAP GTS provides functions including the following:

- Denied Party screening (Customer Master)
- Sanction Country Screening (in transactions, order, delivery, invoice)

- Screening on Products License (Material Master)
- Denied Freight forwarder screening (Vendor Master)
- Dangerous goods
- Harmonized tariff code management
- Drawback functionality

SAP GTS provides import and Export custom related government compliance controls, so that corporations stay up to date with regulations, avoid fines, and penalties. SAP GTM is part of ERP while SAP GTS is part of GRC.

SAP GRC:

SAP GRC stands for Global Risk and Compliance. SAP GRC software comprise of SAP product that is utilize for the following areas:

- Financial Compliance
- Trade Management
- Environmental Regulations
- User provisioning, roles and authorization

Financial Compliance includes SOX, Roles, fraud, and risk related processes. Trade management includes ITAR and EAR compliance.

SAP Activate

SAP Activate represent SAP new methodology gear toward rapid implementation for SAP S/4 HANA. It is primarily driven from agile methodology and aligned with PMI. SAP Activate methodology represented by suite of methodologies based on end result.

1. Prepare
2. Explore
3. Realize
4. Deploy

Phase 1 : Prepare

Prepare phase represent assignment of new governance team. Project governance supposed to be stake holders, architects and project managers. Successful governance team prepare with kick of the project with project vision, scope, resource statement.

Phase 2: Explore

In this phase we start to look into what approach is suitable for the implementation.

Agile Methodology:

Agile is the new emerging methodology. Agile methodology is based on iteration cycles where each cycle feature section of product to test by business users. In each cycle portion of functionality is tested for approval. In each cycle there is business interaction with the system validation also while in the process of testing bugs and errors will corrected. Scrum is one of agile methodology which is also increasingly utilized in software implementation. Scrum gain the popularity due to success rate of the software implementation. Scrum feature deliverables similar to other methodologies however they are delivered in cycles.

ASAP Implementation Methodology:

ASAP stands for Accelerated SAP. It's a project implementation methodology by SAP. It is cost effective, proven, and streamlined for SAP solution implementations and if utilized as it is defined by SAP. It is also called an SAP road-map implementation. The newest version of ASAP is introduced by SAP, but the scope of this book is to understand the basics and brief introduction to SAP. ASAP Methodology Roadmap is divided into five major phases.

5. Project preparation
6. Blueprinting
7. Functional Developer or Realization
8. Final Preparation or goes live preparation
9. Go-live
10. Support

Project Preparation:

Project preparation involves getting ready for the project, commercial discussion, and finalization of SOW or updates.

Project Preparation involves:

- Team and stakeholder identification
- Role and responsibility assignment
- Team building activities
- Process of approval
- Scope and Objective

The scope of the project means what modules, functionalities, systems, and components targeted for implementation. The scope supposed to be very clear, so everyone is working on the same target. Team building activities are required in the discovery phase for team identifications.

Objective:

Based on the project preparation phase, the stakeholder required report is generated. This report is based on business scenarios and how the overall business is looking toward the future state and innovations from the vision statement. The statement for starting the project should be the essential point for all other deliverables, this way the original project statement will not get off track.

Requirements involve gathering and capturing every point that a business requires and categorizing them according the type of requirement needed. There are two parts of the requirement gathering. The first is to write every single one of them down and get validation on them. The second step is to match each system with its capability and evaluate to be part of an existing system. If not what kind of enhancement expected to lay in further categorizes... Then all of the requirements supposed to present to the business with time estimates within the time limit.

The project scope is based on the project statement. The project statements derived from the business vision statement. It expected to be based on infrastructure or software-based requirement.

Blueprinting:

Requirement start with the gathering of workshops. In workshops, business analyst, and consultant capture current processes. The captured business processes the need to be analyzed for fit and gap analysis. The blueprint gathering requires that it start from a standard SAP process. Also that it be compared to AS-IS process to find its best gaps and perform fit gap analysis. Gap analysis is based on RICIFW: Reports, Interfaces, Conversions, Forms, Work flow. The following are a few examples of deliverables from blue print phases:

- Blueprint Documents
- Functional Specification Document

Blueprint Documents:

Many "Topics" able to include in the blueprint document, but several useful topics that supposed to utilize are in template of the project documents. The following are some of the topics supposed to be in a blueprint document. Every organization uses their own and along with their own project standards. The following are some brief topics that supposed to be in the blue print document. The functional specification document is also one of the deliverable of realization phase.

- AS-IS Business Process
- AS-IS process flow Diagram
- Pain points and requirements
- To-be process flow diagram
- To be process details
- Gap-analysis standard or GAP
- RECIF Process
- Business process owner and BA details
- Project name and doc version
- Status of the document with version history
- Roles and Security
- OCM Change Impact
- Feedback from Business

The blueprint should contain feedback from the business and

from project team members. The time and target date supposed to keep in the document so it able to reflect the end date and completion date. A successful blueprint document supposed to easy to understand, after all it will be read by the business team, not by the technical team.

Realization:

The major activities in the realization phase are system configurations, testing, functional specification developments, RECIF developments, etc. Teams start from the system configuration and enhancements. For testing, a test script is executed with test plans and scenarios. The deliverables are for testing the cycle. It is as follows: test plan, test scripts, document user acceptance documents etc. In the realization phase, activities are involved around

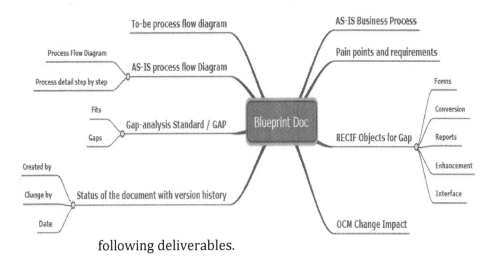

following deliverables.

- System Configuration and configuration
- Testing Scenarios

- Functional Unit testing (FUT)
- Technical Unit Testing
- System Architecture
- Data Migration Documents

Go-live Preparation and Go-live

In the go-live phase, system readiness is tested. In the go-live preparation, data migration is tested in segments of mock testing. Then data readiness and system readiness are tested. In the Go-live phase business process monitoring is one of key activity.

The deliverables and activities involved for Go-Live Preparation phase are the following:

- Fall back Plan
- Data Cleansing and finalization
- Data Migration Mock tests

In the Go-live phase, the deliverables and activities are issue tracking, system handover document(s), end-user support, and planning for long-term support.

Best Practices:

What is best practices? SAP provides industry standards called "Best Practices." The best practices represented the industry's standard utilized by optimized and standardized processed. Best practice given the industry the highest value after international standards of ISO 9000. SAP process and function are based on the best practice.

SAP Best practice represented by standard functions delivered with SAP ERP out of box. To implement best practice SAP building block can be implemented to utilize best practices.

Tips:

- Best practice improve business process

- Best practice also provide industry standards

- Best practices do not require ABAP programing

SAP Configuration:

SAP out of the box requires preparation, with building blocks, it includes business senior and function activations. Building blocks comprise utilize to setup essential baselines of the system. SAP provides OSS notes and documentation for the OSS notes and building block. Configuration for the transactions setup also drive under the term of configuration. The system is configured per business process requirements. Based on the configuration functions of each transaction, the configuration becomes impacted and becomes manipulated. Experienced consultants manage configurations for customization. If the configuration perform without an SAP recommendations and intelligent design, it able to affect the performance and complexity, also making it difficult for the end user transaction.

To configure the system, the T-code follow: SPRO, which is also called IMG. IMG stands for Implementation Guide. Configuration is also called customization.

- Configuration perform by analyst, consultants, and configurators.

- Configuration of customization perform in development first then transported to quality system for additional testing.

- Configuration changes should be considered with best practice first.

OSS Notes:

OSS note stands for Online Service System. OSS represent support system by SAP. SAP provide service pack and version support sustain expiry date of support, then SAP will provide support for bugs or issues throughout OSS. One able to look at subsist OSS notes and apply the solution accordingly. SAP OSS notes able to downloaded and applied via T-code SNOTE. SAP OSS notes system available on sap support websites. OSS notes solution exist for available known issues. These represent the solutions for live bug and their fix patches instructions on how to repair the bug... To view OSS notes, the user require an S- ID which represent a SAP issued ID related to the system.

Tips:

- OSS notes can be searched on https://support.sap.com/

- Obtain a S-ID from SAP Basis or security team

- OSS notes incident support require detail document for SAP to investigate.

EHP:

EHP stands for Enhancement Pack. Each version of SAP follow with many enhancement packs. Enhancement pack provides new features and upgrades to the latest version of SAP ERP ECC.

The latest version of SAP ERP ECC 6.0 enhancement pack "**SAP ECC 6.0 EHP 7**"

SAP Fiori:

SAP Fiori UX personify a revived application that gears toward new mobile user experience. It provides a mobile web base use of ERP functions. SAP Fiori represent a bundle of applications for the enterprise with User interface and customize functions for user specific needs. It comprise compatible with mobile devices and constitute easy to customize. SAP Fiori web base application allows access for mobile device and tablets. SAP Fiori feature released a set of application based on ERP module's functionality.

For more information
http://help.sap.com/fiori_products#section1

SAP Personas:

SAP Personas comprise a screen customization application. SAP Personas built for ERP GUI customization. The customization transactions capable to customized along with scripts that able to integrate into buttons and shortcuts. The background, buttons, themes, and colors capable to customize; it's as easy as drag and drop. It's preface by SAP and will affect all the SAP products for a design change.

Project:

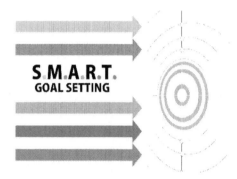

Any strategy or planning that own a beginning and end date able to categorize as a project. A Project feature a project plan, project scope, and resources. A Project is executed with interrelated activities with project implementation methodology. The Project Methodology personify examples of ASAP and Agile.

Any target that is managed under boundaries of time, resource, and scope able to considered a project. Many methodologies represent utilize per recommendation of system integrators and experts. System Integrator represent a reference to the contracting company who come as the contractor's implement, upgrade, or rollout projects. Project excels when project statement and vision is manged and shared with whole team and business.

Origin of Project:
Where cause the project to initiate? The need for improvement, innovation, dealing with subsist issues, system limitation, and

compliance ability represent one of many reasons for the project. The original need is presented to the stakeholder and higher management for approval leading to the project scope thus the approval for project.

Reason of the Scope Issue:
Thoughtful scope able to improve project performance. When the scope is not defined it impact on project performance. Project stay on track with project vision reminder and scope mitigation. Large companies like Google and Facebook represent great examples. They own an open door policy for ideas and issues.

Project Methodology:

What is Methodology?

Methodology represents systematic, organized proven model or method that allows for implementing objectives. Methodology represent a model of work that has been tested and performed many times for expected results. Use of methodology ensures the expected result from desire projects. Use of methodology is proven in many areas to accomplish success in calculating manner.

By utilizing Methodology one able to expect a predictable result. Methodology able to represent effective if followed entirely, otherwise it becomes harmful because a new way of implementation constitute different. Methodology feature a set of rules and parameters with a phase-wise approach. Based on industry best practices, one methodology able to represent more effectiveness as compared to another methodology.

Example of methodologies:

- Implementation methodology
- Business modeling methodology
- Research Methodology

Due to validation by industry standards, methodology use represent one of the deciding factors for controlling the outcome. If the methodology is not followed, then a trial and error cost unpredictable. When individuals or organization deviates from the methodology, that then place the project at risk, thus making it a human error.

Project Phases

What comprise of Project a phase? Project Phase means a limited or defined period of time. The project is divided into phases. In project phases, particular activities are defined for the each phase. The activities and targets require to accomplish before the next phase.

SAP ASAP Methodology

1. **Project preparation Phase**
2. **Blueprint phase**

3. Realization Phase
4. Go live preparation Phase
5. Go Live Phase

Each phase feature deliverables and a set of activities to consider and complete for each phase. Certain methodologies utilize more phases and small, iterative cycles to reach goals. For example "Agile" mythology feature small iterative cycles. What represent a project cycle? Project cycle means the beginning to end of the projects' from the first phase to the last phase of the project. Each phase of the project requires team work with interrelated activities.

Project Issue / Opportunity Management:

What represent the issue and what represent the risk? The issue is already occurring. Risk represent the future state of what is proceed to materialize, however, it allow problem at a later point of time. Every issue is an opportunity for correction. The risk and issue logs supposed to available to project teams and business teams to update. If these logs are not available to the project teams to update, then that ability effect performance of the project. If the issue and risk from the teams are not identified, then the issue will affect later point of the project.

Issue Log:

Issue log is the list of issues where project team track bugs and follow up on them. Project issue logs supposed to follow by a project manager to solve and accommodate the team's issue. Team members expected to create an issue log and update the issue log. All issues expected to followed properly and address properly. Many tools able to utilize to manage issue logs, including software's and tracking sheets etc.

Project Risk Management:

Risks represent predictions of issues in future. The Risk expected to identify in any stage of the project. The biggest risk exist when project managers, stakeholders, and team members ignore the risks. Risk guess calculated with ROI and followed up as per return on investment result. Risk represented in screenshot where man talk on a thin rope, it personify the next step of the project always on risk. Project issues always able to resolve with risk   assessment.

PMO:

PMO stands for Project Management Office or officer. Often times there one project manager from customer side and one from the vendor side. Project expected to feature multiple project managers on both sides accommodate the project. A project manager's responsibility comprise of manage resources, scope and delivery.

Project complete life cycle:

What comprise of a project? The project sustain start and end dates. Based on the project timelines, it feature particular goals and objects that require to accomplish. The best way to attain these targets follow to utilize methodology. After successfully completing all of the required activities from the phase project ends, this then completes the life cycle of the project.

SOW:

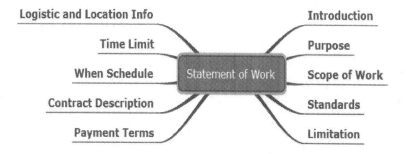

Above figure elaborate on topics from SOW in Mind map

Introduction:

SOW stands for a statement of work. It comprise of legally binding document / engagement / service contract. SOW represent the short form of Statement of work. SOW is result of a bidding process from a request for quotation and negotiation process in between companies to formulate a contract. SOW contains details of project durables score, start and end dates, contract type, pricing, compliance, and detail terms and conditions. SOW topics elaborated in figure of Statement of work.

Description:

Statement of work represent the contract between services providing company. It contains project deliverable. SOW feature high levels of information regarding project durables. During the project if new requirement raised other than project SOW then requires a change request. With a change request SOW requires version management and its updates in project plan.

Lesson learned Project Experience:

In this topic we learn how one able to learn from mistakes and what lesson educated from previous projects. Important it constitute natural phenomena to earn from mistake, but also as human we tend to forget. To learn from past mistake it equal essential to keep a log of issues and mistake to avoided them.

IT Infrastructure:

This is referred to a physical server and network setup of the organization. It contains server software, data centers, network, etc. IT infrastructure also refers to hardware or software infrastructure.

Rationale Document:

A document that contains a pictorial representation with step-by-step instructions is called a rational document. A rationale document suppose provide few or all of these elements: Definitions, instructions, screenshots, procedures, different

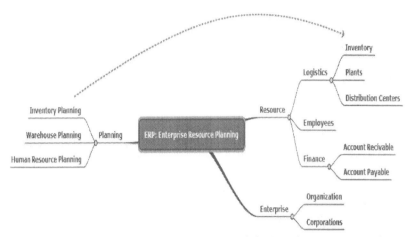

organization, and customization and design documents with their requirements. This document also able to utilize for a training document. Depending on the organization naming convention based on project guidelines.

ERP

Representation of ERP in mind map.

ERP Stands for Enterprise Resource Planning. A few of the ERP functions are defined in figure and show how enterprise resource planning works. Many business departments are managed by the organization, thus the ERP software becomes a necessity that able to handle multiple departments and resources centrally.

Enterprise:

Enterprise represents a business or organization. Any big organization with big departments or many departments able to called an enterprise.

ECC:

ECC stands for ERP central Component. ECC abbreviation employ by SAP to identify its new release of SAP. Usually ECC term practice for SAP version ERP 5.0 ECC OR SAPERP 6.0.

Service Pack:

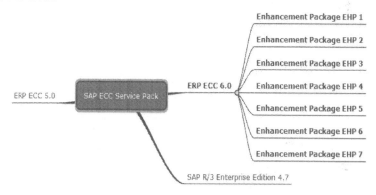

Service pack refers to upgrades to specific version of SAP. The reason for a service pack expected to base on fixing bugs and additional features.

System Landscape:

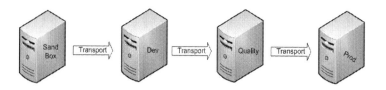

System Landscape

In general, system landscapes own three identical environments. In a project, we develop functions in a "development system" and then it is transported to the "quality server" for testing. After the testing follow practice, it will be transported to the "production system". The sandbox able to also represent a "development system" or a separate system. It depends on company-to-company and how they require to fix the system landscape and sustain how many environments.

The system landscape consists of separate SAP server instances identical and make connectivity for transport requests in between them. In general, system landscapes consist of three system environments:

Development

Quality

Production

Development System:

The development system utilize for system configuration and custom development. Organization to organization system able to subsist in single server or multiple servers. Particular users have selected roles and access to the system. The customization change is assigned to transportation request and these customized objects are transported via transport to quality for further testing.

Quality System:

Quality environment efforts are spent on testing. Quality system users pass or fail test scripts. The quality system is utilized for "user acceptance testing" and "regression testing". Quality environment require to check the quality of configuration and custom development testing.

Production System:

Live systems utilize by business transactions are called production system. Changes to the production system are very limited. For new functions, developments are only allowed in sandbox. The quality system transport follow after the process of approval and successful test cycle completed. Production system requires data migration data before they go-live. End users utilize the production system after go-live.

ABAP:

ABAP stands for Advance Business Application Programing. ABAP employ in SAP to interchange or enhance the SAP standard. ABAP programming language comprise basis of SAP programs. To read ABAP programing, practice the following t-codes. These t-codes also provide examples how to utilize the syntax in programing.

T-codes:

ABAPHELP

ABAPDOCU

ALV:

ALV stands for ABAP list viewer. Most of SAP reports feature an ALV option to select different variations and selection options for the data to display. With this, users able to hide, display, or suppress fields or header and item level information into the report. It's a very flexible tool for reports.

BAPI:

BAPI stands for Business Application Programing Interface. BAPI is also called the functional module. BAPI constitute the programming that enables transaction or master data relevant functionalists for interface users. BAPI used on programs for data loads, interface and enhancements.

Document:

Paper documents records utilized for record keeping. In this day in age records archived in computer files called an electronic document. In computers and servers all electronic files archived in database as electronic documents. The electronic document embody into three sections.

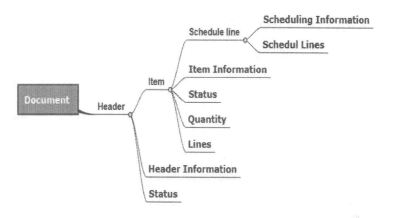

The document represents information or proof record or record.
In a SAP document it feature three parts

1. **Header**
2. **Item**
3. **Schedule Line**

The header represents a controlling point of the document, item represents the content of document, and schedule line indicates its own a particular action at the end of a document.

In SAP SD, each document able to own two to three sections without schedule line, while only sustaining a header and item data information in it.

SAP SD document types:

1. **Sales Document**

Header Data
Item Data
Schedule Line Data

2. Billing Document

Header Data
Item Data

Header Data:

Header data defines the type of document. It controls the behavior of the document.

Item Data:

Item data contains header data and it contains Item data. Each line data feature the same header.

Schedule Line Data:

Schedule Line Data contains scheduling information of a document.

Database:

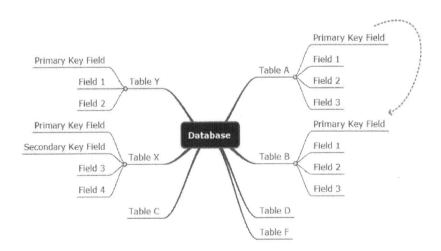

The database represent a repository or collection of tables. The table is consisting of rows and columns. Database is managed in database servers.

Number Range:

Number range controls the number of master or transactional data. Number range represent a SAP configuration for transactional or master data. The series of Number range utilize in different transactions, but mainly two types of number ranges exist:

1. Internal Number Range
2. External Number Range

Internal number range able to utilize for sales orders numbers, customer master, master data objects, or other transactions. Configured number range auto generated by the system. The internal number range configured comprise of as per customizing object. The external number range means that the user able to utilize their own number in the transaction.

Table:

Tables represents data store in the structural way. Tables contain information in rows and columns. Data utilized for programs and software. Where the row and column intersect it's called a field. In SAP, data is utilized for master data to transactional data. SAP feature very large numbers of tables in SAP ERP application. Each field contain its characteristics, for example character types (Numbers or Alphabets) are allowed for what represent the length that is allowed in the field. This represent the information and settings of a table that are stored in "Data type". Every table feature a header data to distinguish this table from other tables and program use.

Every table contain one or more key fields. The key field in the table is utilized to make a connection from data table to data table or make a unique row of data. The purpose of a key field equal to identify the same key filed by looking up data in other tables for relevant information and contribute data with less complex and big data into pieces. In SAP tables represent system-defined tables and SAP allows user to make customer tables. Tables able to produce with T-code SE11.

Key Field ID#	First Name	Last Name	DOB
78692110	Ali	Zer	01/01/82
78692111	Sibtay	Jaffer	02/02/65

SAP feature headers and item tables for different transaction and master data.

Header table and item table connect with each other with key field.

Field:

A field located at rows and column intersection. Each field feature properties for a header field. In other words, if a header field represent date then for each record following this field there supposed to be dated data expected remain consistent. Each field features many controls behind it. Field characteristic defines at header level. The following represent several values of the field.

- Field Name
- Technical Name

- Key Field
- Data Element
- Data Type
- Length
- Decimal Place
- Short Description

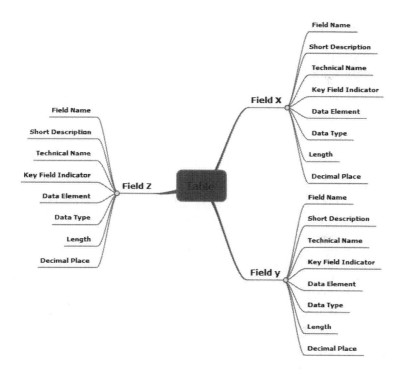

Field Status Group:

SAP feature four field statuses and it called field status group:

1. Required
2. Suppressed
3. Optional
4. Display

With this control, if allowed, each field able to displayed, hidden, suppressed, or optional in the master data or transactional data. The required field status represent a mandatory field. The suppressed field option utilized to hide the field. The optional field property utilized to keep field optional to utilize or leave it empty.

Display:
Display status of the field only displays the content and cannot be changed. When field status represent on display status, it only displays the content of the field.

Suppress:
Suppress means hiding the field from the screen on the master data or transaction data processing.

Optional:
Optional field status is utilized to represent available as an option. When field status represented as an optional, the user able to fill the data or leave it empty in data processing.

Required:

Required field status represent the status of the fields that required for data processing. When a filed represented as on required status, the transaction able to processed unless required entry contain value.

Data in SAP:

The system feature two types of data.

1. Master Data
2. Transactional Data

Master Data:

The data that hardly changes and utilized in transaction as basis for the transactions.

Example and more information:

The name and address of a person able to considered as a master data. The name of a person hardly changes. The address able to represent a master data, and it changes rarely too. In SAP master data sustain many fields to represent its detail. Master data consist on the basis of enterprise structure.

Transactional Date

Data that changes often called a transactional data. Transactional data always based on a master data with variations of transactions. The sales document, delivery and billing document represent good example of transactional data.

Node:
Node refers to computer, server, or a group of servers. The

node utilized in networking terms to define the system.

EDI:

EDI stands for Electronic Data Interface. EDI represent the way that data gets flow between EDI capable to transmit and receive files between them. EDI constitute the industries, standard to send and receive EDI orders, invoices, delivery, and other transactions to manage business.

IDOC:

IDOC stands for Intermediate Document. IDOC's made for EDI interface and interfaces. IDOCS able to viewed with t-code IDOC. IDOC also able to utilized for data migration along with LSMW.

SQL:

SQL stands for Structured Query Language, SQL represent query of database. SQL utilize to call tables and data employ SQL commands. It is based on ANSI.

ANSI:

ANSI stands for the American National Standards Institute. ANSI help in the development of standard, and for more information, please go to the link http://www.ansi.org.

BASIS:

Basis refers to the SAP system admin and security module. A basis consultant installs, upgrades, maintains, secures, and administer the system. The basis consultant role embody to authorize the setup related activities in projects and in system support. Basis analyst also upgrades systems and enhancement packs.

Instance:

Just like a Node, instance is referring to a single computer, server, or group of server define at one instance.

Server:

The server represent a computer that connects via Internet to computers, laptops, and mobile phones to process the application. The server software serves a single or group of systems. In general a server feature more processors, memory, and network bandwidth to process many systems requests.

IP address:

IP stands for Internet Protocol. An IP address is a unique address for each computer or network card. An IP address is issued against the unique Mac address on each network card.

Object:

Word object is also utilized as object oriented programming referring it to the single reusable piece of a program or library. The object is referring to section of complete set of program.

Synchronous Interface:

Synchronous means real time data processing transaction. A good example of synchronous process is when data is synchronous between two or more phone calls. It is utilized in interface related documents if the interface is synchronous.

Asynchronous Interface:

Asynchronous is opposite of synchronous, it is not real time. For example, when the process involves periodic update then it considers asynchronous. It is utilized in interface related document if the interface is asynchronous. For example, mail via postal service takes time to arrive to its destination. .

AR (Account Receivable) and AP (Account Payment):

AR refers to accounts receivable, which is utilized in the revenue for the sales income. AP refers to accounts payable and is in the result of procurement when buying products or services and needs to pay for them.

Accrual and cash Basis Accounting:

In accounting, revenue is calculated on the basis of either cash or accrual. Accrual mean added up and keeping track of it. On the accrual basis of accounting the amount is tracked and eventually it is posted for accounting purposes. Cash basis accounting is posted as soon as the transaction is processed in the system or accounting.

Profit Center:

Profit center is related to accounting, it keeps track for profit and cost. Profit center is utilized in SAP finance and controlling module.

Cost Center:

Cost Center is an internal company account, which is use for accounting purposes to add expenses. Cost centers are utilized to put expenses toward the accounting in order to track the cost of departments. In general, cost centers are utilized for marketing, giveaways, research, development, and return cost tracking.

Process:

Process is an activity which takes inputs, adds value to it, or changes it and produce outputs from it.

Business Process:

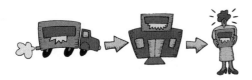

What is a business process? The process feature inputs and outputs with value added to the input. Any inputs are worked on and/or added value to it. From there it produces an output that feature added value to it. If the output is different from the input, then it is called process. Any process of business is called business process. For example, sales order creation is the business process.

Process Flow Diagram:

The pictorial representation of process is called "process flow diagram". The process box is in the rectangular shape that presents a process and it feature input and output. Each process feature value added to each call box, which is a process itself. The methodologies have many representation schemas that represent the process flow diagram. An example of process flow diagram methodology is UML and BPMN. UML. It stands for Unified modeling language, and BPMN stands for Business Process Model Notation.

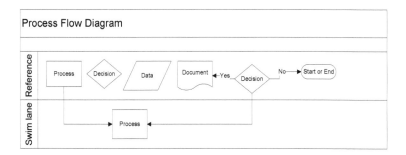

Business Process Methodology:

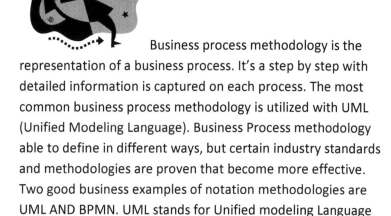

Business process methodology is the representation of a business process. It's a step by step with detailed information is captured on each process. The most common business process methodology is utilized with UML (Unified Modeling Language). Business Process methodology able to define in different ways, but certain industry standards and methodologies are proven that become more effective. Two good business examples of notation methodologies are UML AND BPMN. UML stands for Unified modeling Language and BPMN stands for Business process Language.

Workflow:

The business process feature a process of approvals for quality work and accountability. Workflow is a system of work that goes through business approvals and administration approvals. `Also in SAP, workflow is part of RECIFW that is counted toward system change, other than the standard functionality of SAP ERP.

Use case:

Use case is a pictorial representation of process in framework of representation method. This will help for visual process flow and also help to better to understand. The use case feature Actors in stick figures interacting with system define in the middle. This is UML Methodology is utilized to represent use case. Use case is created per required gathering and documentation for the project.

Use case diagram. It is a simple diagram representing the system and characters.

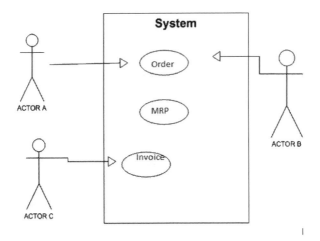

General Ledger Accounting:

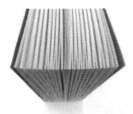

General ledger accounting is an account of all business transactions. GL is utilized for profit, loss report and financial calculation. It is very important for businesses to keep track of transaction for legal and accountability. The SAP feature general ledger accounting is integrated with all of the modules and it keeps track of all financial transactions.

T-Account:

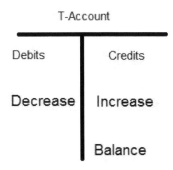

T-account is utilized in accounting. It is utilized for account with journal entries. On the left side of the T-account is debit and on the right side is credit. In the figure above, we able to see that the left side is the debit and that the right side is credit. At the end of the T-account, we able to see balance from both sides of transactions and keep track of journal leader balance with sub T-accounts.

WBS:

WBS stands for Work Breakdown Structure. It is utilized in projects to calculate work, time, and cost relating to the project. It is part of the Module Project Systems (SAP PS) for internal order and project.

Journal entry:

In T-accounting each transaction is entered either on debit or credit, this is what is called a journal entry.

Credit

Credit means an increase in amount or gain. Credit refers to entry in accounting when balance increases. When we over pay our bill then we will receive a credit balance transfer back.

Debit

In accounting, debit refers to the decrease in the account. For example, debit means to pay out something so its decreased amount is transfer out of the balance.

Debit and Credit:

Debit and credit means one party credit is an opposite party's debit. When we receive money it is credit and when we pay it is debited.

Credit and Debit memo

Credit and Debit memo is just a document that is refereeing to the credit and debit in the document.

SME:

SME stands for Subject Mater Expert. Subject matter expert is a title given to technology or business related knowledge.

SAP Consultant:

SAP Consultant is a title for the role in which his/her responsibilities fall into the project implementation or support role.

The responsibility of consulting differs based on organization, the role, and responsibility assigned to him/her, methodology, or organization structures of work.

OCM:

OCM stands for Organizational Change Management. Successful projects and business always pay importance to change management. OCM role is also done by project manager and business analyst so transition to new system go smoothly. OCM streams help businesses prepared for the new system. OCM teams work with management for organizational changes.

Stake Holder:

A stakeholder is an individual or group of individuals who are responsible for the project from the business side. The project manager reports to the, stakeholders for project progress.

Stakeholders able to approve the additional scope of the project or remove it, based on projects vision.

Big Data

Big data considered where an organization feature huge data to process and different tools are utilized for data warehousing and data processing. One of the big data product example is SAP BW or SAP HANA.

"Z" and "Y" customization:

The customizations in SAP are saved with a name or number. SAP recommends customization to start with "Z" and "Y", so it will not be over written in the process of upgrading. By customizing objects saved with "Z" or "Y," it will not be overwritten in the upgrading process.

Role and Responsibility:

Business:

Role and responsibility always defined clearly in successful projects. Role and responsibility personify importance to define clearly in business role as per compliance and regulations.

SAP User:

SAP user are defined with roles and access for transactions. Some transaction allow to change or transaction allow to display only access.

Notes

Chapter 2

SAP Navigation

SAP GUI:

SAP GUI software required to be installed on windows machine in order to access SAP. GUI software represent only a shell, then it required server details to be entered to access SAP ECC. SAP GUI feature option to enabled ECC, SCM, CRM and other components to access.

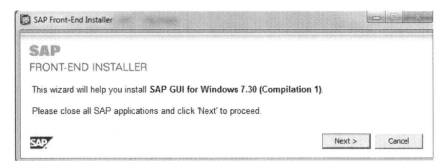

Select the first option from the screenshot to enable ECC access.

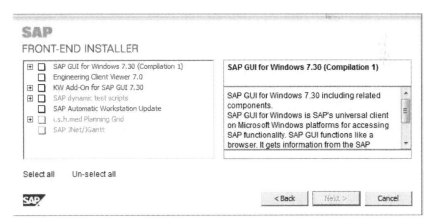

After SAP completely Installed shortcut to SAP GUI will appear in desktop or programs folder.

.SAP GUI Setup:

GUI is a tool to access SAP ECC server remotely. GUI require SAP ECC server details within GUI to access. To setup GUI access open GUI application from desktop icon and click on new connection.

To setup new access follow arrow from above screenshot. Each organization sustain their own credentials to setup for SAP ECC access.

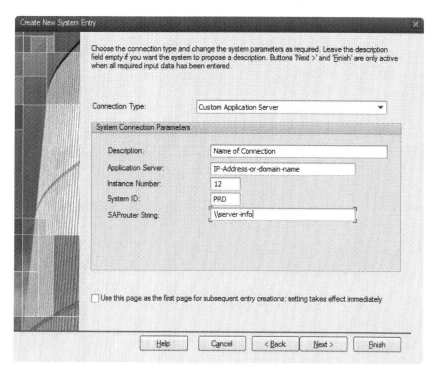

In above screenshot user enter the discription, application server information, instance number, system ID and SAPRouter String. All of the information provided by SAP security team or system admin. Not all f the fields are required based on the setup of oraganization setup may deffer. In some cases user might not maintain this step, all of the setup already populate by SAP basis or security.

After the new setup is made it will be saved in GUI and user can access SAP from using the link. GUI used for SAP Products access including followings:

- SAP CRM
- SAP APO
- SAP GRC
- SAP SCM
- SAP ECC

SAP Easy Access Menu:

SAP Easy Access Menu represent the initial screen after logging into the SAP GUI. SAP Easy access menu feature SAP menu to display different function and application areas for users to look in their functional area.

- The easy access menu easily customizable with GUI options.

- In general the SAP easy access menu allow six separate sessions open at same time.

- The easy access menu feature a transaction bar code bar T-codes.

- The easy access menu can be customized and assigned to the user or to a group of users.

- SAP Easy access menu feature SAP menu and favorites.

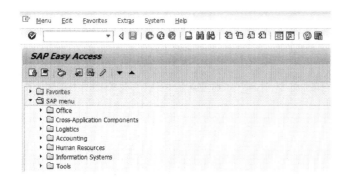

T-code:

T-code stands for transaction code. The easy access menu feature a transaction bar, as seen in the screenshot. In this transaction bar a user entered a T-code.

Tips to remember T-code:

Here are some tips to remember T-code alphabets.

Character	Description
N	Number
V	Sales
F	Billing
M	Material Master
01	Create
02	Changes
03	Display
05	Report

To get reports for any module from EASY Access Menu use T-code: **SAP1**
this will only show a report from every module.

For sales related MENU use t-code: **VA00**

T-code Bar:

T-code bar represent a bar where user enter transaction code (T-code). There is also small triangle that close the T-code bar. Alternatively user can use folder structure to drive into the folders to run the transaction.

Transaction Code Short Cuts:

From transaction code bar user use following short cuts to process transactions.

/o	Open New Session	Ctrl + O
/n	To end the current transaction	
/i	To delete the current session	Alt + F4
/nend	To log off with saving	
/nex	Exit without saving	

Tips: Most use shortcut is "/n" to end current session. User use next T-code after "/n" ending current session. For example first user review the customer master and from same screen user would like to view sales order. In order to

/n(t-code)

Example:
/NVA03 (t-codes are not case sensitive)
Use short cut to end current session and enter the next t-code after the shortcut:

/*(T-code)

when "/*" is used it will skip over the first screen to enter values and press enter. It can be useful with combination of parameter and last entry from transaction. For example if use saved a sales order then use /*VA02 to go into change sales order directly.

SAP Copy Past:

In SAP copy, past function work with command "Ctrl + Y", and it display plus sign to text to be selected. User can copy text by scrolling over and select "Ctrl + C". Text past with "Ctrl + V".

Select Text   =   Ctrl + Y   " **+** "
Copy   =   Ctrl + C
Past   =   Ctrl + V

Easy Access Menu buttons and shortcuts:

Button	Description	Shortcut
	Enter	
	Command Field for T-codes the triangle close the command field	
	Save	ctrl + S
	Back	F3
	Log Off (from current session)	Shift + F3
	Cancel	F12
	Print	Ctrl + P
	Find	Ctrl + F
	Find Next	Ctrl + G

Button	Description	Shortcut
	First Page	Ctrl + page up
	Page up	
	Page Down	
	Last Page	Ctrl + pg den
	New Session	Ctrl + N
	Create shortcut	
	Help	F1
	Customize Local Layout (change Color, themes, font size, etc.)	
	Add to Favorites	Ctrl + shift + F6
	Delete Favorite	Shift + F12
	Change Favorite	Ctrl + shift + F3

SAP Messages Types:

SAP error messages are defined in different categories. Some errors are not able to bypass. If a warning which is normally red comes on, it means it's a hard error and cannot sustain to ignore. Not all errors are not hard errors, these errors are called soft errors. The warning error color is yellow and it able to ignored, however the user will see warnings. In the event that the transaction system issues a message, it means that the status of transaction changed by the user. An SAP, messages is defined in different categories, with their own message types. Each process feature a message type in SAP. It gives a status to the user that results in success and failure:

1. Warring
2. Error
3. Exit
4. Success

Each process feature a message type in SAP. It gives a status to the user that results in success and failure.

SAP Massage Type

Message Type	Icon	Description
Information		The message type is for information purposes, by clicking the icon it will open a new window with information.
Warning:		It feature warned you on the next step. It able to correct before the warning is ignored. (The user able to ignore it by pressing enter) The warning may appear more than once based on transactions. It appears on left bottom of the screen.
Hard Error		Message gives a hard stop. Unless the correction is made, it will stay at error and will not process.
Exit		Message exits the trisections and gives a short dump, or stop the transaction.
Success		Success message with document number or if this transaction is successful this will appear. It appears on left bottom of the screen.

Changing GUI Color

User able to change color of SAP GUI from selecting customize local layout (Shortcut Alt+ f12) and then select options.

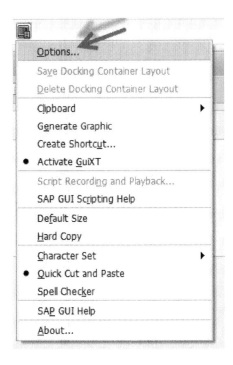

By Selecting different options user can select different colors.

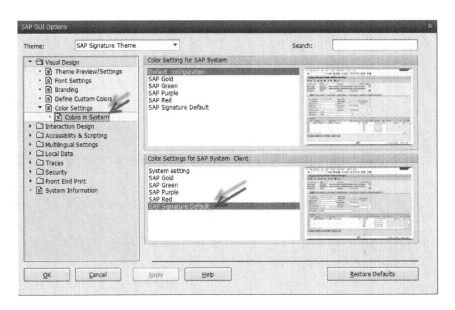

After the changes click on Apply, user required to open a new session to view new color or might require to completely log out and log back in in SAP GUI. The selection colors are provided by SAP are following:

- Gold
- Green
- Purple
- Red
- Default (Blue)

Quick Copy Past

User ale to activate quick copy past option for SAP GUI. With quick copy, past every time user select text while holding mouse left button system will copy the text and when user like to past just click on right button of muse and system will past the copied text.

Please review the screenshot how to activate

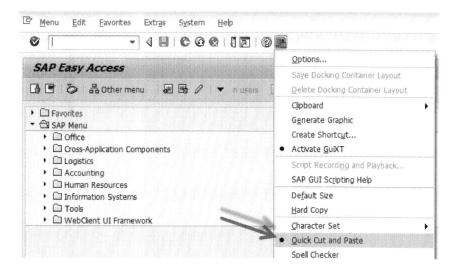

SAP allow special clipboard options to copy and past function. User able to select text by special select function "Ctrl + Y". When user enable select function system will display plus sign "+", then user can scroll over the text and select the text. After selecting simply copy by "Ctrl + C" and past with "Ctrl + V"

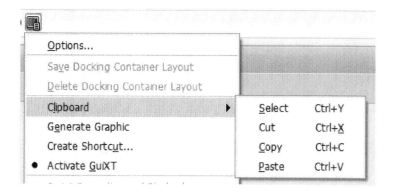

SAP Print Screen:

User able to print current transaction into printer by selecting hard copy option. By selecting hard copy current screen will processed to local printer for print.

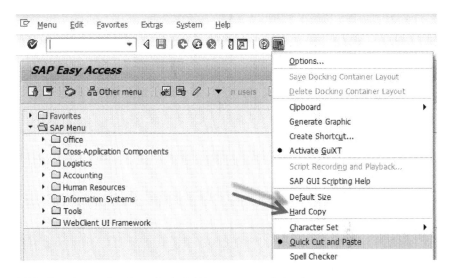

This function print the whole SAP screen on the printer.

Transaction Desktop Shortcut

User able to create shortcut based on single transaction code. Simply navigate to the transaction or move to favorites and right click on the transaction and click on

Add Favorite T-codes:

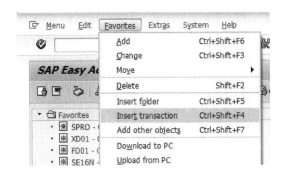

Enter Transaction code to add the transaction to the favorite.

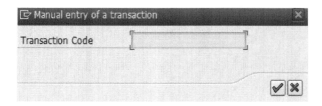

User able to download the Favorite list and save as .doc or .xls or .txt or .html or .RTF file formats. The favorite list can be uploaded into new GUI.

T-code Name Display:

To make t-code more meaningful one make their description display in favorites. Added transaction code do not display description of transactions. To display description one can enable the function for user.

Select Extras from manu → Setting

Sortcut: Shift + F9

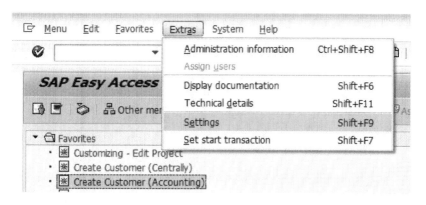

Click on checkbox option of "Display Technical Names"

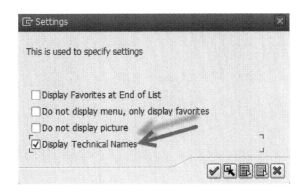

By selecting this option all of the t-codes will displayed favorites. This also assist users to remember transaction codes.

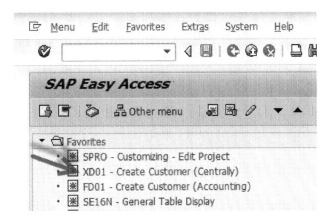

Above screenshot display t-codes with discription.

Personalize and Defults Setup

Date format:

User able to setup date format as per country or the way they need to control the date on SAP transactions. Different date format required when users are in different countries and they utilize different date format.

How to setup date format?

Use T-code: **SU3**

Or follow the screenshot

User Profile → Own Date

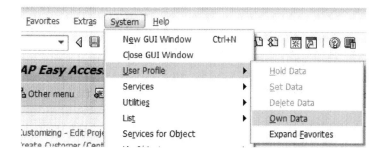

Seect defult folder.

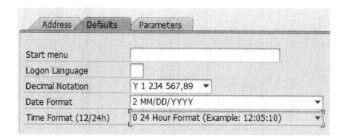

Automatic Populated Values

Values can be auto populated for transactions in SAP. We can setup auto populated field by setting up parameter in user profile.

Parameter ID Automatic Defaults:

User can setup defaults based on Parameter ID. Parameter ID represent technical name of the field that can be defaulted automatically when user use a transaction. For example when user try to create customer master Sales organization "Z110" will be copied to sales org field.

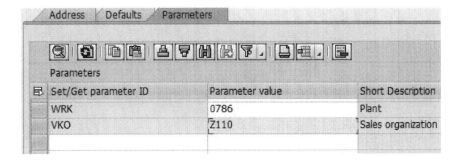

In above screenshot plant made to default values of "0786". When user enter transaction code where it require plant to be entered default plant will be promoted automatically.

Users can sustain parameter ID and default values to be determined.

List of useful parameters:

Parameters used in user profile to auto populate entries in transactions.

Parameter ID	Description
BUK	Company Code
CAC	Controlling Area
VKO	Sales Org
KPL	Chart of Account
VTW	Distribution channel
SPA	Division
WRK	Plant
GSB	Business Area
PRC	Profit Center
FIK	FM : FM Area
EKO	Purchasing Org

Display Dropdown Keys:

User able to select an option to display key for the drop down list of options. It is universal activation if the list contain key for the list then key will display front of it. Please review the screenshot how to activate the keys for the list. It is also useful for

Step one 1

From SAP Easy access Manu or from any SAP access screen select on option.

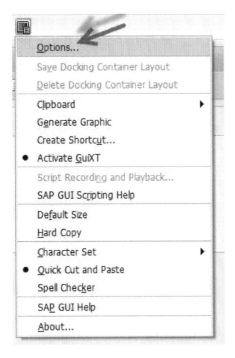

Step 2

Select Interactive Design folder and under it select visualization 1 Check mark on Show Keys within drop-down lists.

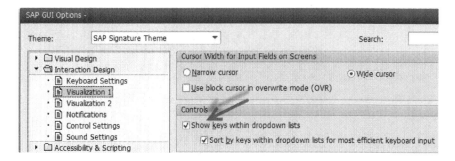

The change may require log user to log out of SAP GUI completely and log back in or in some cases may require computer restart for change to take effect.

Search Transaction Code

To search transaction code user can click on search icon or select shortcut: "Ctrl + F" for search single entry.

User can enter transaction code to search. User also can search from transaction code texts. To search text it would be recommended not to use asterisk before and after texts.

To search similar transaction code click on search icon with plus icon. Search icon to find next in search click on binoculars with plus sign from screenshot. Shortcut to find next select: "Ctrl + G"

With simple search user can also press on press icon to search next available transaction code.

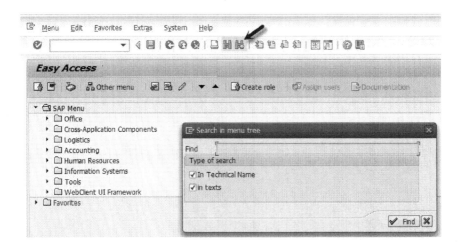

SAP GUI contain two icons for search transaction codes. First icon of binocular represent search icon for first find search. Next Icon of binocular icon feature plus sign in it to find next available search result. For next search option keep clicking on the button to find next search result.

One more way to search transaction code is by transaction.

T-code: SEARCH_SAP_MENU

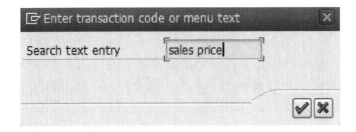

Result for the search result with transaction code.

Node	Transaction code	Text
Nodes	MEI7	Adjust Sales Price
Preceding node		Automatic Document Adjustment
Preceding node		Follow-On Functions
Preceding node		Purchase Order
Preceding node		Purchasing
Preceding node		Materials Management
Preceding node		Logistics
Nodes	VKP2	Sales Prices
Preceding node		Environment
Preceding node		Promotion
Preceding node		Environment
Preceding node		Bonus Buy
Preceding node		Conditions: Sales
Preceding node		Condition/Arrangement
Preceding node		Environment
Preceding node		Vendor Rebate Arrangements
Preceding node		Subsequent Settlement
Preceding node		Master Data
Preceding node		Purchasing
Preceding node		Materials Management
Preceding node		Logistics
Nodes	VKP8	Sales Price Calculation
Preceding node		Environment
Preceding node		Information System
Preceding node		Environment
Preceding node		Material Groups
Preceding node		Environment

Show Keys in Dropdown List:

By default users cannot view the key values in drop-down list. With enabling of option of drop-down list view users can view the keys with in the list from drop-down list of selection.

First select option button and select on options.

From options user can enable show keys within dropdown keys.

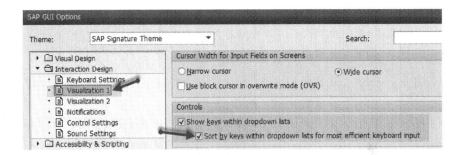

Default language dropdown without keys

Dropdown   with   keys   displaying

Chapter 3

SAP Reports and Layout:

ALV:

ALV stand for ABAP List Viewer. ALV utilize for report in SAP. ALV allow user to customize the report. ALV report contain set of function provided by SAP for reports. Following are functions provided by SAP for ALV.

- Download Local file in Excel/HTML
- Sort the report in Asending and Desnding
- Save layout for he reports
- Subtotal and Totals
- Adjest report columns to hide and dispay

SAP Report Selection:

In SAP entry user can add report t-codes to the favorites but also there is one shortcut. With shortcut T-code all of the reports will display as per module.

Transaction code: **SAP1**

After entering t-code user need to drilldown per module to review available reports.

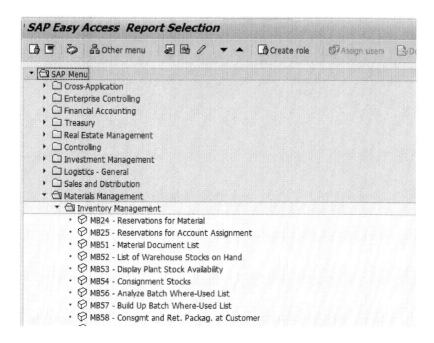

User can click on modules or area for the avalable reports or worklists.

Reports:

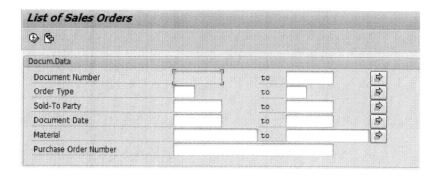

Report function contain "From" and "to" limit search in sequence only. This function is very useful when user are searching in between dates, or number in sequence with first and last number.

Multiple Selection can be entered by multiple selection icon, from screenshot. There is also exclude single values or exclude range can be entered.

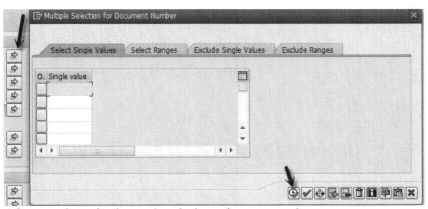

After entering selection and exclusion select execute icon.
Based on values report will include and exclude from selection options.

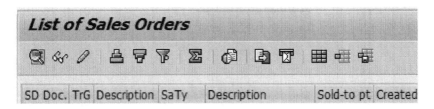

All fo the filter options are defined further with deails.

View from Report

 Glasses are good hint to remember that icon used for view document from report.

User first select line item from report resuksult and then click on

Change from Report:

Pencil mean this document can be chnaged from report

Simply select the line items and click on change icon from report. If the "pencil" function available it may allow changes from report. Change function may not be available for all of the reports. User may require change access to also for this function to work.

Shortcut Ctrl + F11

Report Ascending and Descending:

△ Sort in Ascending Order
Shortcut Ctrl + F4

▽ Sort in Descnding Order
Shortcut Ctrl + F5

First select the column to be in ascending order then click on icon for ascending or descending order display, also similarly select on ascending to update report.

Description	TrG
Sales order	0
Sales order	0
Sales order	0
Sales order	0
Sales order	0
Sales order	0

Please find additional interactive assending and desending steps in "**Report Customization**" section.

Filter in Report:

▽ Shortcut   Ctrl + F5

Filter function allow value or values to filter from report. Filter feature also function with more one column at a time.

Please find additional interactive "Filter" steps in "**Report Customization**" section.

Total in Report:

Σ Shortcut   Ctrl + F6

SAP "Total" function only works for the field where values can be calcuated to total. First select the field that required for for total and select total icon or (Ctrl + F6). Ttoal will display in the end of the report summing up the whole value.

Change Layout

Shortcut   Ctrl + F8

Layout represent favorites arrangement selection of columns. User can save as many layout in SAP and to view different arrangement user change the layout to bring desired report result. SAP user can save their own user layout for user specific or global for all users.

User can select the fields from column set to Display column to display selected fields.

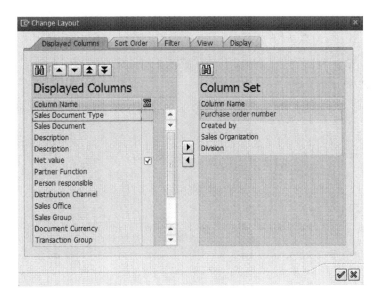

Save Layout

After changes are made for the report, user save the desired view into layout. Saved layout utilized for report view. Select save layout button and name the layout starting with "Z" and write description in name field. Layout also can be default layout upon running the report by selecting check box for "Defult setting".

Shortcut   Ctrl+F10

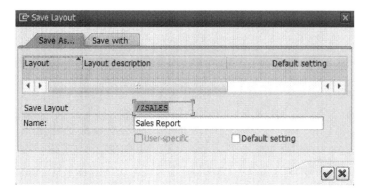

Select Layout

Each report contain multiple layouts. Saved layout selected from select layout icon. Click on "select icon" and select from available layouts in the list.

Shortcut   (Ctrl + F9)

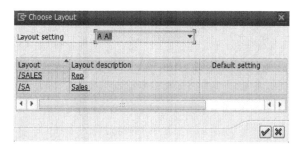

From above screenshot displa avalable layout to be selected.

Download Local File

Shortcut: Ctrl + Shift + F9

SAP reports can be downloaded into local file. Files are available in following formats. Some report contain external file format to MS Excel format.

- Unconverted
- Text with Tabs
- Rich Text
- HTML Format
- In clipboard

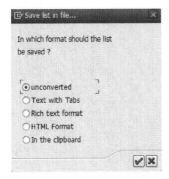

Above screenshot display avalable formates for user to save local file fomates.

One more way to download

from report screen user can select on System → List → Save → Local File

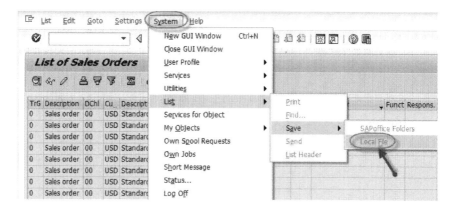

Files can be saved into local file.

Print Preview

 Shortcut (Ctrl + Shift + F10)

Each document print preview display the output from the transaction. This function may not be available from all of the report. If print preview available then it will display the available transaction.

Report Customization:

Reports in SAP has interactive function to

- Hide
- Show
- Optimize with
- Freeze to Column
- Sort Ascending
- Sort Descending

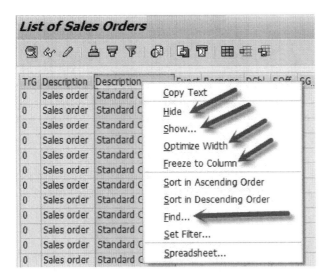

In above screenshot user can right click on column to select options.

About The Author

Syed Awais Rizvi

Syed is a senior SAP Sales and Distribution consultant and experienced with worked in numerous implementation projects. He has years of experience in the automotive, healthcare, security and various industries. Syed Awais Rizvi serves as the Chief Executive Officer of ITSAS LLC.

SAP Certified Sales and Distribution Consultant.

SAP Certified Project Manager.

IBM Certified System Administrator

Kindly leave a review on Amazon.com

Connect with author for feedback and comments rizvir@gmail.com

Subscribe @ http://phtime.com/ for updates!

Thank you

Made in the USA
Middletown, DE
07 March 2017